I0802716

SAFETY CHECK

HAZARDS

Written by
Valerie
Harvey

KidHaven
PUBLISHING

Published in 2027 by
KidHaven Publishing, an Imprint of Greenhaven Publishing, LLC
2544 Clinton St., Buffalo, NY 14224

Written by: Valerie Harvey
Edited by: Noah Leatherland
Designed by: Jasmine Pointer

Cataloging-in-Publication Data

Names: Harvey, Valerie.
Title: Hazards / Valerie Harvey.
Description: Buffalo, NY : KidHaven Publishing, 2027. | Series: Safety check | Includes glossary and index.
Identifiers: ISBN 9781534570702 (pbk.) | ISBN 9781534570719 (library bound) | ISBN 9781534570726 (ebook)
Subjects: LCSH: Safety education--Juvenile literature. | Accidents--Prevention--Juvenile literature.
Classification: LCC HQ770.7 H378 2027 | DDC 613.6071--dc23

Printed in the United States

CPSIA compliance information: Batch #CS27KH: For further information contact Greenhaven Publishing LLC at 1-844-317-7404.

Please visit our website, www.greenhavenpublishing.com. For a free color catalog of all our high-quality books, call toll free 1-844-317-7404 or fax 1-844-317-7405.

Find us on

Image Credits:
Cover - KOTOIMAGES, IQ art_Design. 4-5 - Ground Picture, fadfebrian. 6-7 - Miljan Zivkovic, ProShine Studio. 8-9 - Ruslan Huzau, Mashala S, Yauheni Kazlou. 10-11 - Prostock-studio, Pressmaster, Doodling Poe, cool vp, nik_nadal. 12-13 - FotoDuets, Art_Photo, Technicsorn Stocker, Doodling Poe. 14-15 - Monkey Business Images, tomeqs, K-FK, Krumani. 16-17 - DGLimages, FamVeld, IQ art_Design. 18-19 - Kostikova Natalia, Yaoinlove. 20-21 - Melnikov Dmitriy, Ola List, Tanysl. 22-23 - Anatoliy Karlyuk, Red Fox studio.

All images courtesy of Shutterstock.com, unless otherwise stated.

CONTENTS

Words that look like this can be found in the glossary on page 24.

WHAT IS A HAZARD?

A hazard is anything that could hurt you if you're not careful. Hazards can be big or small, easy to spot or hidden. A puddle on the floor, a wobbly chair, and even a toy in the wrong place can all cause accidents.

Don't worry, though! When you learn how to spot and prevent hazards, you can stay safe and help others stay safe too. Let's find out more about what kind of hazards are out there.

Spotting hazards before something goes wrong is a great skill.

HOT, COLD, SHARP, AND SLIPPERY

Some hazards are things we are around every day. Hot objects, such as cooking pots or ovens, can burn us. Very cold items, such as ice packs, can also hurt our skin.

Sharp objects, such as scissors and knives, can cause cuts. Slippery surfaces, such as wet floors, can make us fall. When we know what these hazards are, we can make smart choices to keep ourselves safe.

THE POWER OF ELECTRICITY

Electricity makes lights shine, TVs work, and devices charge. But it can also be dangerous if we don't use it safely. Electrical sockets, broken wires, and overloaded outlets are hazards. They can cause shocks!

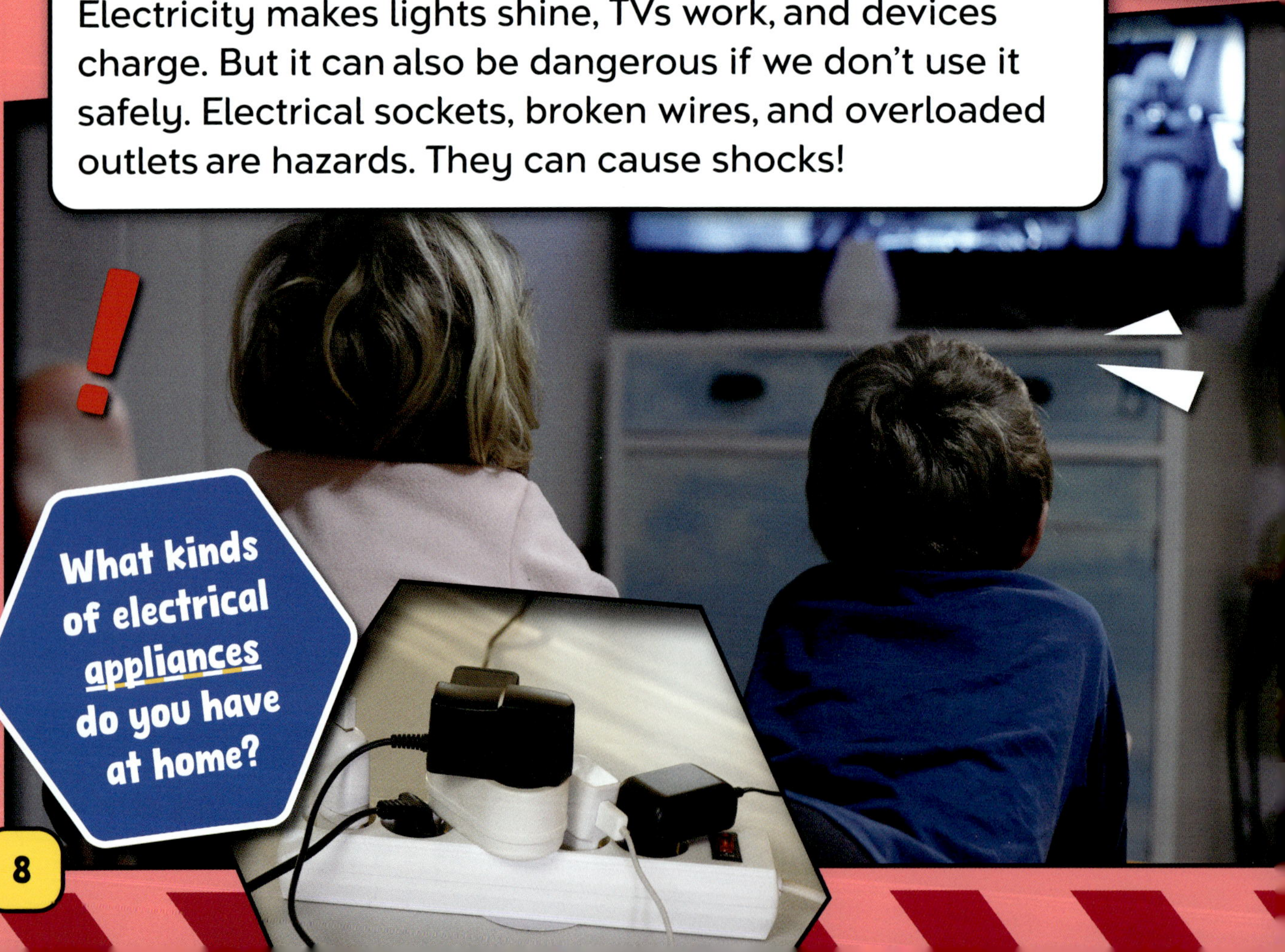

What kinds of electrical appliances do you have at home?

We should never touch electrical things with wet hands or poke objects into sockets. When we treat electricity with care and follow safety rules, we can enjoy its power while staying safe.

KITCHEN CAUTION

The kitchen is full of exciting sights and smells, but it's also a place to be extra careful. Cooking uses lots of tools that can be hazards.

Always ask an adult before using kitchen tools. With smart choices, the kitchen can be a safe place to cook, learn, and help!

Only use kitchen tools with an adult's permission.

BE CAREFUL OF CHEMICALS

Cleaning and garden products often use chemicals. Chemicals help keep our homes clean, but they can be harmful and make us sick if they touch our skin or mouth. Never open or touch chemical products unless a trusted adult tells you it's OK.

When we respect chemicals and use them safely and carefully, they can do their jobs without causing harm.

Bottles containing chemicals should be stored safely.

OUTDOOR ADVENTURES

Playing outside is fun, but it's important to spot hazards in nature too. Uneven paths, loose stones, and muddy patches can make us trip or fall. Some plants have thorns, and some insects might sting or bite.

By being careful about where we walk, climb, and explore, we can enjoy the outdoors safely and make every adventure a great one!

Sunburn is also a hazard. Hats and sunscreen help keep us protected.

LOOK, LISTEN, THINK!

Crossing the street has many potential hazards, so always be careful! Stop, and look both ways a few times. Listen carefully for cars. Only cross when it's safe.

Streets often have a specific place where people are supposed to cross, such as a crosswalk or traffic light. Use these crossing areas to help you stay safe.

Wearing bright clothes in the dark helps drivers see you and keeps you shining safely!

SMALL HAZARDS

Tiny things can cause big problems. Small toys, buttons, and coins can be dangerous if they're stepped on or put in mouths, ears, or noses. By paying attention to the little things around us, we help everyone stay safe and happy.

It's important to put away toys when you've finished playing.

Little things left on the floor are especially dangerous for babies or younger kids because they are a choking hazard. Keeping floors clear means fewer hazards for everyone.

Choking is very serious. Always tell an adult if you see someone struggling to breathe.

PLAYING SAFELY

Playtime is a lot of fun, but staying safe helps the fun last longer. Before you start, check your space. Are there toys on the floor you could trip over? Are swings, slides, or bikes being used carefully?

Playing safely with others helps prevent bumps and falls. Remember to follow the rules of games and wear any safety gear you need, such as helmets or pads. When we play with care, everyone can enjoy the good times together!

YOU'RE A SAFETY STAR!

Being a Safety Star means using everything you've learned to look out for yourself and others. You can spot hazards, make smart choices, and know when to ask an adult for help. Safety Stars don't panic—they stay calm, think clearly, and act responsibly.

Can you be a Safety Star?

Whether you're at home, at school, or outside, your safety skills shine bright. Keep practicing, keep noticing, and keep caring. You're ready to stay safe every day!

GLOSSARY

appliances devices that do specific jobs

chemicals substances that materials are made from and that can affect how something works

choking being unable to breathe because of an object stuck in the throat

prevent to stop something from happening before it does

INDEX